Questions

On Topics That Matter

The ABC's of How To Live Life Better

Vicki K. Silverman

Testimonials

Vicki Silverman draws upon her vast experience and wisdom as an educator to encourage readers to examine their thinking, patterns, and interpersonal dynamics in a relevant, at times humorous, and user-friendly book. Rich with artistic touches of original poetry, this thought-provoking gem opens the door for exploring how to live a richer, more mindful life. Invoking real-life situations and dilemmas, her book offers an invaluable, manageable process for teachers, therapists, individuals, parents and teenagers, couples, women's groups, and businesses that want to review priorities, values, and relationships.
  -Audrey S. Foote, MA, MFT

Reading through my lens as a Doctor of Clinical Psychology in private practice, I became excited and inspired to see such a wide range of subjects covered in the form of questions designed to lead a person towards deeper self-discovery. This book is for clinicians, lay leaders and individuals seeking answers to questions about who they are and how to find more meaning in their life in the present as well as on their journey into the future. I will not only use it personally, but in my practice with clients as well. If this sounds like something you are seeking, you will find it a wonderful tool.
  -Dr. Pam Sirota, Psy D; MFT, former teacher and school director

Ms. Vicki Silverman's *Questions on Topics That Matter: The ABC's of How to Live Life Better* guides readers into their own introspection, whether they take individual journeys or work together within groups. Chapters include Silverman's own poetry, thought-provoking scenarios, and questions for discussion and/or journaling. The author's choices of topics help us explore our own challenges and questions in a spiritual quest toward our authentic selves. Her book is similar to a 'coffee break for our souls,' assisting us in ultimately acquiring the joy and wholeness that we all seek and deserve.

-Dr. Barbara Jaffe is a fellow at UCLA's Department of Education and is the author of the 2017 memoir, *When Will I Be Good Enough? A Replacement Child's Journey to Healing*. Jaffe is also a regular contributor to *Psychology Today*.

Questions On Topics That Matter:

The ABC's of How To Live Life Better

ISBN: 9781790116584
Imprint: Purple Stone Press

A Thank You

*To Ken, for your consistent love and support of what
I choose to do and for always making me feel
Loved and valued*

*To my children Julie and Scott, for giving me the family
life I always wanted and for choosing spouses, Andy
and Kaci, who so perfectly complement
each of you and complete us*

*To my grandchildren, Emma, Jake, Miles, and Zack for
bringing me more joy than I could have ever imagined,
not to mention more gift wrap, candy, and jogathon
fundraisers than there are grains of sand
in your shoes*

and

*To my extended family, incredible friends and
occasional perfect strangers who are
unsuspecting triggers for much of my writing*

Table of Contents

Prologue, Prelude, Preface, Forward, Backward, Inward, and Ongoing

Today and every other day, errands, technological challenges, demands and needs of others, and the prevalence of controversial world news lurk around every corner. At some point, we may wonder how to balance everything and go to sleep feeling a sense of satisfaction that it has been a good day.

Exactly what can we do about it? Adults give children "time outs" when life gets out of hand. In the *LA Times*, Jan.3, 2015, Marc Brackett, Ph.D., Director of the Yale Center for Emotional Intelligence, calls this "a meta-moment, the "space in time between when something happens and we react." Children are advised to take a deep breath and think about what has just happened. How many adults do that? How many of us really take the time to consider the bigger picture and strategize what to do next?

What happens when life feels too complicated? How do we find a true sense of contentment in our everyday existence? Young parents, after all, methodically go through each day overseeing the daily needs of their children. Others balance business demands, time with family and friends, and outside interests. We get to meetings where and when we need to; we manage homes, bills, text messages, blogs, and complex daily schedules. Then, we go to bed exhausted, fall asleep (or not), and wake up the next day, wondering, hmmm, what was yesterday all about?

What if we could consider the issues we face, and, at the same time, challenge ourselves from within? How could we do that and what would that look like?

Imagine meeting with a small group once a month, at someone's home or through an on-line group, all bringing different life experiences and expertise to the talks. Or, if you prefer to do this by yourself, envision thinking about the topics in the privacy of your home.

Dedication

This book is dedicated to the twelve women who have been meeting and sharing in monthly conversations that have led each of us to living a more meaningful life. I treasure you all for your combined poise, presence of mind, insightful take on life, logic, warmth, sincerity, calmness, wisdom, grace, class, encouragement, soulfulness, questioning minds, heartfelt interest in each of our perspectives, kindness, and genuineness. I am forever grateful for the synergy of our group, which is empowering, timely, and treasured.

We are the collective minds that gather to think about how the world works and what our roles are as we walk our own ever dynamic and unique paths. We are Anita, Barbara, Ellen, Frima, Joyce, Mady, Teri, Marlene, Rusty, Sherry, Terri, and myself, Vicki.

Dear Reader,

Just a note as you start this journey. Time for yourself is so important and this is an opportunity for you to do just that . . . set aside time for yourself. You may open each conversation by reading and considering my poem at the beginning of a topic. Then reflect on one or more of the scenarios and finally start to examine the questions.

It does not matter how many questions get answered; it is about generating an open conversation with yourself or with others and being amazed at where it will go. It will often take on a life of its own and you may sometimes find the questions helpful simply as a backup tool.

Enjoy!

Vicki K. Silverman

The Beginning

What is your style? Are you more comfortable with an internal dialogue or in a group setting? Do you think you would benefit from exploring life's quandaries by yourself? If so, explore the topic choices that follow.

Decide which one seems the most relevant to you at that moment. Then put yourself in the scenarios and imagine how you would handle each situation. Start asking yourself some of the questions that follow and consider how you might answer them. Try to be instinctual in your responses; this is a time to explore your inner truth as it comes forward. Ask what you can learn about yourself by exploring your emotional and ethical reactions to the questions. Are they different? Is there a difference between a knee jerk reaction to a situation and an ethical consideration? No answer is right or wrong; it is your truth and only yours.

Or, would you benefit from first contemplating a particular topic, asking yourself a few questions and then following up by having a conversation with a friend?

Finally, if being in a group suits you best, gather together some people you would like to spend time with and get to know better. It should be made up of a "safe" group based on specific criteria for selecting members, including but not limited to such qualities as open-minded, curious, kind, respectful, willing to invite differing opinions, sensitive to another's perspective, and non-confrontational. In addition, think about the diversity of your group, considering age, race, religion, sexual orientation, etc. Some groups work well when they share similar backgrounds, while others thrive on diversity. A more eclectic group will generate discussions that reflect the varied backgrounds of the group members.

Begin by initially inviting 2-3 people who you think would enjoy conversations about universal questions. Ask each of these people to think of another person or two to add to the group; after you all agree on the people to add to your group and are confident they each align with your pre-determined criteria, invite them to a first meeting. A total of about ten members becomes a "community" of your collective making.

This book can be utilized, explored, and delivered in a variety of ways. Choose which means suits your life best. Take as much time as you want to consider the perceptions you have and the reality you live each day. Then, think about making changes so that you can, in fact, live the life you dream for yourself.

More than a Conversation

<u>Meeting 1</u>: Set up the ground rules for your group

★ Get acquainted, define your personal goals, and form common goals as a group.

★ Establish the day, time, and location to meet once a month (for example, first Tuesday of the month at 1:00; rotating homes each month takes the burden off of any one individual).

★ Determine how you are going to select topics and who will lead the discussions, either the host/hostess or anyone in the group who wants to lead that month. The leader can research the topic ahead of time for background and can decide whether or not to bring a printout for the others.

★ Establish parameters for the discussions (such as decide whether or not to allow politics, religion, and personal experiences).

★ Consider refreshments, and if so, how minimal or extensive.

★ Give an assignment for the next time you meet, such as, "Think about any positive influences in your life (not people) and bring a book, poem, art, or article to share that has positively influenced you in some way."

★ Finally, ask everyone to turn on their radar for interesting topics. Discussion opportunities are everywhere…in magazines, newspapers, television, radio, the internet, and the conversations of others. Designate a folder for notes or articles to collect ideas for future topics.

PART 1

Become Who
You Want to Be

Finding My Focus

Amidst crowds, clutter, distracting conversation,
All the mixed messages and uninvited intrusions
Of everyday life,

I find time to think, opportunities to be mindful,
To choose my own path,
To become the master of my own life,

Living for this moment only,
Aware of my choices of
How to be present in whatever I do.

Chapter 1
Act Mindfully

Scenario 1: Bev is at a restaurant sitting next to a parent with his eight-year old child. Both are on their cell phones. She notices that no conversation takes place for at least ten minutes. What is wrong with this picture? How could the parent and child mindfully connect?

Scenario 2: You are driving home after a long day of work, and though it seems that you have just stepped into the car, you have already been driving for twenty minutes and are pulling into your driveway. It feels as though no time has passed. Were you thinking about something in particular on your way home? Were you thinking at all?

Questions for Discussion

Do you tend to function automatically and robotically in your everyday life? How so? What do you do each day that puts you on automatic pilot?

Describe how people today tend to multi-task or schedule their days with back-to-back activities.

What happens when you feel stressed from being busy? Do you have a constant stream of ideas in your head? What does that look like? Do you ever feel emotionally drained?

Consider this quote by American writer, journalist and cartoonist Allen Saunders from *Reader's Digest* in "Quotable Quotes," January 1957, and later repeated by John Lennon: *"Life is what happens while you are busy making other plans."* How can that happen?

Are you able to quiet your mind and become present? If not, what can you do to be more mindful? How can you change your day to be the master of your life and define how you are living? These changes do not have to be grand; think of what small actions or behaviors you can change, eliminate, or add to your day to help you live in the moment.

Where do you think you can practice mindfulness?

Zen Master Thich Nhat Hanh, global spiritual leader, poet and peace activist suggests that "the most precious gift we can offer others is our presence. When mindfulness embraces those we love, they will bloom like flowers." Are people present when relating to others? If so, describe it; if not, describe how that might look.

If we are feeling angry, do we necessarily have to pass that on to whoever is around us? Or, could a shift in our perspective help? Do we need to change our filter? Can we let go of the anger in order to be present for others? Consider what brings you joy and comfort and what you need to do to achieve it.

According to Thich Nhat Hanh, "The present moment is filled with joy and happiness. If you are attentive, you will see it."
What do you think of that concept? Does that mean that there are no sad moments if you just give the present moment your full attention?

Is mindfulness about figuring out how to be happy?
Complete the following sentence:
Mindfulness can create a world where you experience _____ and _____.

Is thinking mindfully mostly about changing your attitude, judging your thoughts, or about being aware and accepting them?

We live in a technological world today with information disseminated in many ways, often leaving us feeling over-stimulated yet sometimes yearning for even more. How does that work against our attempts to live "in the present"?

How does authenticity relate to living mindfully?

What benefits could you reap from living more mindfully?

Relate the concept of "quality" not "quantity" to mindfulness.

Reflections

_____

_____

_____

_____

_____

_____

_____

_____

_____

_____

_____

_____

_____

What to Say, What to do, For You

At times, without intent, I find myself
Surrounded by meaningless chatter
A discord of jumbled sounds
Disturbances and unwanted invasions
That try to silence my devotion.

I inhale deeply and then exhale slowly,
Once again hearing background sounds,
A peaceful paling of commotion
As I begin to hear my inner voice
Beneath all the uninvited noise.

What to say to you, what to do for you
How to nourish your needs, sometimes over my own,
To love, accept, and support your dreams and visions,
To champion you and always see and hear you.
So that you know you are loved, valued, and heard.

Chapter 2
Become Spiritually Nourished

Scenario 1: Jane has trained for the marathon for six months post cancer treatment. She is excited to return to her passion of running. When she is midway on her run, she twists her ankle, comes to a painful halt, and cannot continue. What reactions could she have to this potentially devastating moment? How could she help herself? How could someone give her the spiritual nourishment she needs? What could bring her a smile?

Scenario 2: Irene is dating John, a health enthusiast, who eats an inordinate amount of carrots per day. He even has them delivered once a week! John is, however, singularly focused on whatever he does, and it is not on the people with whom he spends time. He keeps his body fit, but he is turning orange from his carrot diet, and his relationship with Irene is going nowhere. What is missing from his "diet"?

Questions for Discussion

Describe a situation that might make you feel emotionally raw or hurt.

Do you know how to love yourself? What does that look like right now? What do you do for yourself when you are in pain?

Sometimes people unintentionally impose their own obstacles that prevent them from personal growth. Is this a reality in your life? What might keep people from feeling spiritually nourished?

If you could wish for emotional support from a parent or friend when you are suffering, what would you hope that person would say to you?

Consider writer, poet, lyricist, and family and marriage counselor Rusty Berkus's list, "The Voice of Your Inner Benevolent Mother," from *The Diamond of the Soul-Six Facts for Living Your Life with Dignity:*

1. I will love honor and cherish you throughout this lifetime and all other lifetimes.
2. I will love and accept you for your strengths as well as your weaknesses, your shadows as well as your sunlight, through your victories and glories, as well as your disappointments and defeats.
3. I will support, empower and strengthen your Spiritual Starhood and magnificence.
4. I will forever support your dreams and your visions.
5. I will always see you; I will always hear you; I will cry with you in your pain and sorrow; I will share and revel in your joy and fulfillment.
6. I will always respect your humanness, and your need to take care of yourself.
7. I will do everything in my power to bring peace and harmony into your consciousness.

8. I will always be there for you, for you are unabandonable; you are lovable, no matter what the appearance or situation.

9. I have every confidence in your choices and decisions.

10. I will never allow anyone to abuse you in any way.

11. I will do everything in my power to promote your very highest good, and to ensure that you are treated with Dignity.

12. I will always remind you that you are enough, so that all you need do is breathe and be, with no expectations.

Did you get this nourishment from your parents? If you did not, could you gift these qualities to yourself? How would that look?

The Golden Rules tells us to treat others as you would like them to treat you. Imagine another way of looking at it: Treat yourself as you like to be treated. Could you do that?

What are some initial thoughts and feelings one could have if wronged by an acquaintance? Insulted by a friend? What could you say to yourself to turn these feelings around?

Do you know people who seem to want to sabotage your success in some way? What does that look like? If so, should you completely disconnect with them or are there other ways to deal with that person (co-worker, a boss, a relative, or anyone in a position of authority)?

What should a friend provide in a friendship that would "nourish" you in some way? How could you reverse this to nourish them?

Do you think you have empathy for others? If so, how? If not, what can you do to tap into their feelings and give them the gift of understanding?

If you feel spiritually nourished and give off positive energy, how does that affect those around you? Also, does that work in reverse? If you give off negative energy, how do others treat you?

Does technology have any effect on spiritual nourishment?

A thought: "If you can't get a compliment any other way, pay yourself one."
~Mark Twain, American author

Reflections_____

_____

_____

_____

_____

_____

_____

_____

_____

_____

_____

_____

_____

_____

_____

_____

Mixed Messages in the Mirror

I reflect and what do I see
Disappointment looking back at me.
I just can't get it right.
I am a failure in plain sight.
I missed my chance.
I'm too old now to take a strong stance.
I am not smart enough.
I am damaged, not tough.
I don't have enough time
The mountain's too high to climb
I can't risk another failure
I just need to do better.

I blink and what do I see
Positivity looking back at me.
You are loved and radiate dignity
You value peace and harmony
You are supported and cherished by your friends
Good choices and decisions are your bookends
You are precious and kind
Keeping others keenly in mind
You are who you are
You are enough, a superstar.

Chapter 3
Control Negative Self-Talk and Nurture Positivity

Scenario 1: Marsha attends a law office party where she knows no one except the office manager, her neighbor. She doesn't like large groups, feels anxious, and is painfully aware that she knows nothing about law. How can she navigate the party and cope with her feelings?

Scenario 2: A colleague has just been given a promotion that you feel you deserve. How would you be inclined to interpret this situation? What would you do? How would you feel? What would the dialogue in your head sound like? Do you see yourself as a victim and would your self-esteem be affected? Or, would you try to justify the decision in some way or look at it differently?

Questions for Discussion

If you are bombarded with negative thoughts, is it possible for you to change or make a paradigm shift in your thinking?

What do you say to yourself when you are self-criticizing? In what areas do you think you are "not enough"?

Complete this sentence: I don't think I _____ enough.

How do you see a raised self-esteem increase your confidence level?

What happens when you pass judgment on something in yourself that you cannot change (such as aging, your height)? How is this helpful?

Why do you think people talk so much about themselves, their joys, challenges, and mundane everyday experiences in social media? Are they bragging? Is it pleasing to them? Or, is it something else? How do you react when reading such entries/declarations?

What do you feel negative about when it comes to yourself?

Have you been judgmental or negative about anything in the past day or two? What was it?

We often allow our inner critic to bring down our self-esteem. We all have imperfections. What are yours? Can you live with your imperfections? How would that look?

Consider focusing on "progress" rather than "perfection." How might that look?

Can you define what makes a person "enough"?
Author and holistic living educator Krista O'Reilly Davi-Digui writes in the article, "What if All I want is a

Mediocre Life," that all she wants is "…a small, slow, simple life…and to be left in the space of in between." She feels it is enough. Do you agree with her?

How powerful is attitude? Give examples of situations you have known that show the power of attitude when people have been faced with challenges.

What do you find helpful and hopeful about yourself? That is, if you send yourself positive messages about yourself, what do you send and how does this feel when doing so?

What is something you are working on to improve?

At times we have insights into our inner selves. How could we turn our desire for positivity into actual actions?

If you start the day with negative thoughts, how do you foresee your day evolving? What can we gift ourselves when we do not feel we have enough or are enough?

Imagine waking up in the morning and having a plan for positive behavior for that day. What would your plan be? What simple things could you say to yourself or do to make it likely you will have a good day? Where might you be? Who may benefit from your positivity?

Consider something you did today or yesterday that you felt good about. What was it? Who has been by your side and encouraged you in some way?

What if you get in bed at night and have negative thoughts? Do they keep you awake? How can you redirect these negative feelings? Would it help to listen to music? Read? Get up and organize something? Watch television? What else might help you? Some say to avoid all technology after 7:30 p.m. What do you think of that idea?

What do you think of the impact social media has on our self-esteem?

Do you think that women are more self-critical than men?

What are some ways you or people you know feel regretful or disappointed? What has led you or others to experience this disappointment?

Do you know people who chase what they don't have and not pay attention to what they do have? How can there be power in letting go of the chase to be enough?

A thought: "A smile is an inexpensive way to improve your looks."
~ Charles Gordy, British army officer, Crimean War

Reflections_____

_____

_____

_____

_____

_____

_____

_____

_____

_____

_____

_____

_____

_____

_____

_____

Beneath the Mask

Hidden faces
Covered by happy coconut smiles
Unfeeling distortions
Plaster of Paris frowns
Distinctly unique masks
Ceramic statements
Handmade, machine made
Assorted sizes, shapes, and colors
Timeless textures
Hiding, protecting what's real
What feels the joy and pain
Hidden
Beneath the mask.

Chapter 4

Define Your Authentic Self

Scenario 1: John is a politician. He is vehemently opposed to a policy his party favors. Should he publicly make a statement in favor of or in opposition to his party's position?

Scenario 2: Ila has been raised to value higher education and to pursue a career as a doctor or lawyer. However, she feels a strong pull to enlist in the military and train to fly a fighter jet. Does she listen to her parents or her own inner voice? Explain what you imagine her thinking might be.

Questions for Discussion

When do you feel your most authentic self and are most connected with yourself? Describe what you are doing.

What is one thing that has impacted you and changed you forever (positively or negatively)? How has that contributed to or deterred you from being your authentic self today?

Do you care what people think of you and what you are doing? Do most people?

When you look in the mirror, what do you see physically?

What do you like about your inner self? What do you want to change?

For a moment, strip away your role as daughter, mother, son, father, employee, wife, husband, partner, volunteer, or friend. Now, ask yourself and answer these questions:

* What do I enjoy doing?
* What do I value?
* Do I like new experiences?

If your responses would differ from the answers others might give, would you care?

Should you ever compromise in order to fit in? If so, when?

We all have an authentic self that sometimes struggles with our invented self. When does that happen to you?

People sometimes smile even though they are sad. Is it ever okay to put on a façade? Do you think it helps you feel better or make it worse because you are not dealing with your sadness? After all, the brain does have connections.

We have been told the right way to behave by parents, teachers, spouses, friends, the Bible, etc. Can that make us afraid to be our authentic selves?

Create a list of what you do not want to be. On the opposite column, list what you do want to be. Then, ask yourself, "Am I living the life that is true to myself? Become an archeologist of your genuine self. What needs to be done to find who you are? Think of at least three ways you can unearth your true self. What can be gained by figuring this out? What can be lost?

Are you ever satisfied with yourself? Are you ever "good enough"?

Is social media used as a yardstick for self-image and the ability for one to be authentic? How so?

American author Joseph Campbell advises in *Reflections on the Art of Living: A Joseph Campbell Companion*, "We must be willing to get rid of the life we've planned, so as to have the life that is waiting for us."
What is he suggesting? What do you think?

A thought: "Who is more foolish? A fool or the fool who follows him?"
~ Alec Guiness, English actor

Reflections

Wise Up

What's really important?
The goods that we possess?
Or the people we care about
A word of love, a caress?

Possessions that bring us memories
Are not as precious as
The people and the moments
Of life's ever present past.

Hold onto recollections
Reach for tomorrow's dreams
Use these obstacles that interfere
To help see what is unseen.

Chapter 5
Embrace Wisdom and Aha Moments

Scenario 1: John is working on his car but is having no luck getting it started. His neighbor suggests having the car towed to the nearby mechanic. John responds by saying that he knows what he is doing, but five hours later, the car still won't start. John does not have the knowledge he needs for this repair. Why is his neighbor a wise person?

Scenario 2: Marcus has been working as a lawyer for six years. Even though he went to law school, passed the bar, and has been dedicated to his career, he cannot help but remember that he has always wanted to be a teacher. He has an "Aha" moment while driving home one day from work, realizing he hates his work. What do you think he should do about his dilemma?

Questions for Discussion

What are qualities of a wise person? Complete this phrase:
A wise person understands that _____.

If you could send words of wisdom to your past or future self, what would they be? Begin with the phrase, "I have learned to…" and verbalize a list of what you would include.

Discuss the meaning and value of any or all of the following words of wisdom:
* ✷ Look for balance.
* ✷ Learn for discovery.
* ✷ Never give up; twists and turns often lead to something better.

* Look for the goodness in everyone and everything; seek positive energy.
* Focus on people, not things to do or multiple accomplishments.
* Attitude is a best kept secret; control it or it will control you.
* It is not what happens to people that is important; it is what they do about it.
* Be sure your intentions are reflected in your behavior.
* Feel free to plan but do not believe you are in control of it all. Be flexible.
* If you are born with a gift, it is what you do with it that counts. Embrace it.
* If you think something nice about someone, tell that person or forever regret not doing so.

How do you recognize wisdom in others?

Agree or disagree: People who stay connected to others demonstrate higher levels of wisdom than those who are more isolated.

Discuss what would make the world a better place.

Greek philosophers Socrates and Plato felt that the only true wisdom is in knowing that one knows nothing. At what age do you think most people might agree with this?

We each create our own wisdom as we learn from experience. Describe an experience in your own life that has made you wiser.

Have you ever found good in something that initially appeared to be bad? Describe that moment.

Moments of challenge may lead to a sudden revelation. Think of a moment in your life that felt freeing (a perceptual shift) because you suddenly realized something you thought you had understood but hadn't.

Do you think that you can train or influence your brain to allow you more "Aha" moments? If so, how would that look?

Dr. Celeste Campbell, a neuropsychologist in the Polytrauma Program at the Washington, DC Veterans Administration Medical Center, defines neuroplasticity as follows:
> ... the brain's amazing capacity to change and adapt... as the result of our interactions with our environment... the actual generation of new brain cells.

Relate neuroplasticity to the possibility of "Aha" moments.

Some people tend to nurture an attitude of openness; that is, they want to know more, experience more, and are prepared to be moved by as many things as possible. Do you think they would have more "Aha" moments than others? Are they wiser because of their attitude of openness?

Reflections_____

_____

_____

_____

_____

_____

_____

_____

_____

_____

_____

_____

_____

_____

As the Curtains Opened

Looking back, from childhood through her teens,
She reflects on a home of challenges
Feelings of insecurity and embarrassment,
And no contentment as she gazes about,
Nothing inviting about those dark velvet chairs
Nothing pleasing as she imagines
An uninvited friend's stare.
An eerie presence clothed this home
An inexplicable dark energy
Is all she found as she walked around.

And then, as time moved forward,
On to her own happy, little house,
Her own family and her own parenthood
Nothing formal, nothing grand,
Simply the evolution of color and comfort
Making her feel at ease in her grown-up life
A refreshed sense of self and fulfillment
Inviting her to welcome each new day.

Chapter 6
Find Inner Peace and Balance

Scenario 1: James is carefully driving along and a car speeds by, cutting him off. Initially, he is irate, curses, and gestures wildly. Is this the best way to react? Respond? Does he feel a sense of inner peace and balance afterward? What could be a healthier response?

Scenario 2: Peter has yelled at people recently. He gets impatient quickly. On top of that, he is watching the time at work and feels intensely eager to get home from work each day. What is wrong with this picture?

Questions for Discussion

Do you argue often or like conflict? If so, how does that affect your sense of inner peace?

What do you need to let go of in order to feel inner peace? Answer each of the following:
* I positively do not want to be

_____.

* I feel anxious when I

_____.

* I worry about

_____.

Do you judge others by your own standards? Do you interpret the actions of others? Do you personalize their actions? If someone is acting unkind, does it necessarily mean that person is trying to personally harm you?

What else could be going on?

Now consider what you positively <u>do</u> want to be. Give five characteristics/qualities to describe yourself.

It could be said that we should join our highest intentions with our best actions. How might that bring our inner life into harmony with our outer life?

Describe what you think inner peace looks like. Finish these sentence starters:
* Inner peace is a tendency to think and act

  _____.

* Inner peace is the ability to

  _____.

* Inner peace is letting go of

  _____.

Inner peace is directly related to having a sense of balance in our life. Stop and ask yourself each day, do I feel balanced right now? If you answer no, how can you bring balance back into your life?

Ask yourself, when have I felt most balanced and at ease? That is, when has everything felt aligned and you have felt optimistic about what was to come?

When tragedy, divorce, or illness happen, you may feel a sense of imbalance. How can you get back into balance?

One chooses how busy, challenged, or social to be. Is finding balance generational? Is it different for a man or a woman?

How is setting realistic goals in a career, social life, or family related to maintaining stability in life?

Is it okay to be out of balance? Can you tell yourself, "And this too shall pass. Tomorrow will be a better day"? Or, would that lead to letting go of your goals?

What could happen if you remain out of balance?

What actions could you take to bring balance or self-care back into your life? Be specific.

Reflections_____

_____

_____

_____

_____

_____

_____

_____

_____

_____

_____

_____

_____

_____

_____

_____

Open Your Eyes

Make a mistake? Just close your eyes
Make it seem like it never happened
Let the moment just go away
So that in your heart alone that misstep lies.

Make a mistake? Feel the guilt and shame
For causing others harm
Or breaking your own moral code
Keep it to yourself, for you must be to blame.

Make a mistake? Be motivated to change
And make better choices
Life is trial and error after all
Accept responsibility, keep that finger pointing
Out of range.

Chapter 7
Grow from Mistakes and Guilt

Scenario 1: Laura has a four-and-a-half-year-old child, three-year old twins, and a five-month old. She's trying hard to be a good mother. Her partner works away from home seven days a week and Laura works two days from home when she has a babysitter. She never thought she would yell at her children, but it seems as though she does it more and more, even though she feels horribly guilty about it. What is she probably saying to herself? What should she tell herself to handle the guilt she is experiencing?

Scenario 2: Peter and Mary's son James spiraled out of control from his use of drugs and alcohol and dropped out of college. Sadly, he eventually overdosed. Out of fear or feelings of helplessness, his high school friends had long since stopped hanging out with him to avoid being involved in his situation. They find out that James overdosed, and they feel they made a huge mistake by not helping him more back in high school. What could they do with the regret and shame they are now feeling?

Questions for Discussion

True or False: There is perfection.
True or False: Mistakes, big or small, are not intentional.
True or False: All mistakes can be fixed.

Think of a time when you said something to someone that may have been rude. Describe what it was. Did you do anything to rectify your mistake?

When you make a mistake, what do you do? What are three or four actions you could take that might be helpful?

Can you be a good person and still use poor judgment?

Is there power in making mistakes? What are some positives about making mistakes?

An anonymous quote, "Mistakes are proof that you are trying," examines a positive side to making a mistake. If you make a mistake, is that what you would say to yourself?

It is said that the famous inventor Thomas Edison stated the following when he worked on the light bulb: "I have not failed 10,000 times. I have successfully found 10,000 ways that will not work." What do you think Edison is saying about mistakes? Is this the way you try to look at your own mistakes? Can you use his philosophy when the mistake involves a personal interaction?

French author Jules Renard wrote, "If I were to begin my life again, I should want it as it was. I would only open my eyes a little more."
What does he mean?

What part does regret play in your life?
A. None. **B**. Some **C**. A lot.

What are some positives of regret? Negatives?

On an average day, what do you feel guilty about?

What happens when you have a particularly rough day,
your friend asks you to help with some task, but you
feel you have to deal with your own issues and needs
on this day rather than address your friend's needs? Do
you later have feelings of guilt?

Have you ever wanted to make someone else feel
guilty? If so, describe it. Did you achieve the desired
effect? How did you feel?

Reflections

_____

_____

_____

_____

_____

_____

_____

_____

_____

_____

_____

_____

_____

_____

Happiness From the Beginning

Pink plastic teacups
For her two small guests
Invisible delicacies
Made with great care.

The sound of mom's high heels
Her beads and her bangles
Gestures of a princess
Manners of a queen.

Busy days, quiet nights
Bedtime stories of faraway lands.
Cuddly bears, soft fluffy fur
Kisses good night
Upon rose petal skin.

Then, years later, elegant fine china
Befitting treasured friends
Choices abound amidst the afternoon
Of many voices.

Comfortable cushioned pumps
Simple gold chains
Elegance of wisdom and
The beauty of time.

Lifetime memories tucked in sleepy lined eyes
Cool pillows, a fluffy full quilt
The comfortable caress
Of happiness within.

Chapter 8

Harness Laughter, Humor, and Happiness

Scenario 1: Robert is watching a television show with friends and laughing wildly yet no one around him is laughing. How can that be explained? What might cause someone to not find humor in something?

Scenario 2: You recently watched a politician refer to and ridicule on television a woman he knows. People behind him were laughing. How would you feel watching this?

Questions for Discussion

Laughter is closely associated with comedians. Is laughter closely associated with happiness?

What can lead to laughter?

Finish these sentences starters:
* ✱ I laugh when

 _____.

* ✱ I rarely laugh at

 _____.

What are the benefits of laughter, both physical (one's immune system as well as the effect on endorphins) and emotional?

What might be social benefits of laughter?

Have you laughed today?

When is laughter NOT funny?

What does it mean to have a "good sense of humor"?

Would you consider having a good sense of humor a character strength?

How could using humor make others feel good?

Can humor be used negatively? Think about jokes and media that stereotype or target specific groups (races, genders, or cultures). Consider cartoons that display violence against animals or people. Have you seen attempts at "humor" that are not really funny? How do you respond at those moments?

Is humor generational? If so, how? If not, why not?

What makes people "happy"? Create a list of possibilities.

What makes you happy?

What choices could you make to create more happiness in your life?

Pursuing happiness can backfire as stated in the following quotation (sometimes attributed to Thoreau, Nathaniel Hawthorne, as well as a newspaper called

The Daily Crescent in New Orleans, Louisiana, in June 1848):

> Happiness is like a butterfly;
> The more you chase it, the more it will elude you.
> But if you turn your attention to other things,
> It will come and softly sit on your shoulder.

Does it seem wise to pursue happiness based upon this quote? Do you think it is wise to pursue happiness?

According to Gregory Benford, physicist, educator, and author, "A truly happy person is one who can enjoy the scenery on every detour"? Is that realistic?

Reflections

_____

_____

_____

_____

_____

_____

_____

_____

_____

_____

_____

_____

_____

A Moment in Time

What do you fear?
Pain, danger, a threat
Like a dog chasing you or
A car hurling towards you
Being assaulted or robbed,
Losing the power to control your life,
And today,
Facing unfriendly international relations
Or a bomb set off by terrorists
In our own country or abroad?

Or, are you afraid of Disappointment,
Failure, Rejection, Loss
A devastating illness
Or being alone
Taking risks
Changes in the future
Artificial intelligence perhaps
Taking over the human side
Of our everyday life?

Use that fear to make the choice.
Follow that inner sense of knowing.
Don't back away to safety.
Step forward into the
Face of threat and do something
No matter how big, no matter how small
To triumph over
That larger than life force
Real or imagined.

Fear can hand us control,
Give us our own voice,
Help us summon the courage we need
To move forward
To do something positive and reassuring
Freeing us from our fear
For that moment in time.

Chapter 9
Interpret Fear and Courage

Scenario 1: Marie routinely drives to work and arrives at eight in the morning. This day, though, as she is driving, a car is coming toward her at a high speed. She quickly pulls over to stop her car and avoid being hit. What could she be experiencing at that moment?

Scenario 2: Jason finds out that he has Stage 4 cancer. How could fear affect him? What might he be thinking? Doing?

Questions for Discussion

Fear can be specific or global. How?

Can fear be reality-based as well as unrealistic? How?

What are some common fears that people have?

What are some reality-based fears that you have?

What is your greatest fear? How do you deal with it?

Can a person let go of an emotional response to an actual threat? What can one say to calm oneself?

What are the benefits/dangers of realistic fears? Of fears we fabricate in our minds?

What fears do you have that you cannot really explain?

How can the love of other people make you deal with a fearful situation?

President Franklin D. Roosevelt declared the following in his First Inaugural Address:

> ...the only thing we have to fear is...fear itself, nameless, unreasoning, unjustified terror which paralyzes needed efforts to convert retreat into advance.

Was that realistic advice?

What do you understand by the phrase, "You are not your fear"?

Do women have more fears than men? Explain your answer.

What does fear have to do with control?

How can one overcome fear and be courageous?

Why do you think people resolve to "stay in their comfort zone"?

People have courageously recalled harrowing stories of survival during disturbing moments in history. Discuss a few.

What is courage? Do you have to climb a mountain, run with bulls in Spain, or fight off a would-be thief to be courageous? Think of some difficult everyday moments that people face which require them to have courage. Describe them.

Courage…is it contagious? What could that look like?

Fill in these blanks:

* I wish I would have been more courageous when

_____.

* From now on, I am going to

_____.

Reflections

_____

_____

_____

_____

_____

_____

_____

_____

_____

_____

_____

_____

_____

The Stars Are Out

Consider…
The young soldier who dedicates his life to his country
with unrestricted patriotism…

The teacher who inspires the uninspired student to be
the best he can be
and his best is truly good enough…

The environmentalist who cares about
how and what he discards
where and when and for what purpose…

The passerby who, upon noticing a confused elderly
woman examining a sales slip as she exits a store,
asks to assist
and interprets her itemized receipt,
quelling her confusion…

The girl who cares about the feelings of all
who feels pain and happiness,
even when caring is unpopular,
for doing what is right is not always popular…

These are some of the people who inspire us
to strive to be better
the precious jewels of a tiara,
the brilliant stars we wish upon at night.

Chapter 10

Journey to Inspiration

Scenario 1: Janis manages a great deal of personal anxiety, depression, and past trauma as part of her life. She is also a respected musician. How might she be considered an inspiration?

Scenario 2: Ms. Leeson is an elementary school teacher who offers to visit every one of her students' homes if they would like her to come. She feels strongly that it is helpful in establishing a relationship with them and their families. What is your reaction to her offer? How might she inspire others?

Questions for Discussion

Who has inspired you (in your own life, as well as outside of your own world)? Explain what positive qualities they possessed.

Has someone helped inspire you to overcome a significant struggle?

Have you been inspired to act? What has your being inspired led you to do?
Complete the following:
I was motivated by _____ to _____ after _____.

Who inspired you in your youth from their character role on television or in movies? Explain why or how for each. Do you still find inspiration from them?

What can you do in your everyday life to nurture your ability to be inspired?

How can being inspired by someone ultimately lead you to a different behavior?

Think about the following people (some may call them past and present heroes): Leonardo da Vinci, Steve Jobs, Elon Musk, J. K. Rowling, Nelson Mandela, Abraham Lincoln, Mozart, Oprah Winfrey, Indira Gandhi, Marie Curie, Ruth Bader Ginsburg, Mohammed Nasheed, and Picasso.
What qualities do they share that inspire people?

Do you think that your lifestyle can affect your sense of inspiration? If so, how? If not, why not?

How do you think you have motivated someone (a child, grandchild, friend, relative, stranger)? Explain.

Can you recall a time you have helped someone take a positive step towards a better life?

Consider these movies. Did you find any of them particularly inspirational, and if so, how?
  * *Rocky*
  * *Shawshank*
  * *Forrest Gump*

- *Slumdog Millionaire*
- *Good Will Hunting*
- *Eat, Pray, Love*
- *Billy Elliot*
- *Life Is Beautiful*
- *Rain Man*
- *Hidden Figures*
- *Gandhi*

Reflections

_____

_____

_____

_____

_____

_____

_____

_____

_____

_____

_____

_____

_____

_____

_____

Wondering

Are you curious?
Where did we all come from?
Adam and Eve, a scientific phenomenon
Another planet, another dimension?
None of it makes much sense and the experts disagree.
Will we ever know?

Are there other realities out there?
Look up at the night sky; the world looks so vast.
Is what we see, hear, and feel our only reality?
Why don't we know
And when will we know and how?

Chapter 11

Know the importance of Curiosity/Wonder

Scenario 1: A woman has worked at the same job for twenty years and is getting bored. How could she make the job more interesting for herself?

Scenario 2: You are having an ordinary day filled with the same activities and errands you run every Tuesday. How could you think about that day in a new way?

Scenario 3: When Jill was five years old, she thought about where the universe ends. If it ended with a brick wall and she chipped off the wall, she thought there would just be more universe. Does this childhood wonder cease to exist in adulthood?

Questions for Discussion

Do you think you have a sense of wonder? Are you curious? What do you wonder about?

Many children are very curious, which is confirmed by their unending "why" questions. Adults, though, sometimes stop asking questions. How do you nourish your curiosity? How could you have new eyes to see the world around you? It could be as simple as getting up earlier than usual and seeing what is happening outside or what the quietude is like for you.

Scientists are characterized by curiosity and wonder. They notice occurrences in the world and then ask such questions as, "Why is it that way?" and "Why does it do that?" and "Why did that happen?" What would you ask about? What do you wonder about?

Have you wondered about any of the following:
* What would it feel like to not worry?
* Was the majesty of mountain ranges planned?
* How do people "invent" new things...planes, the fax machine, or rockets into space?
* What would it be like to see a dinosaur walking around?
* Are there aliens?
* Is there a real Bermuda Triangle?
* Is there reincarnation?
* Are there humans like us outside of Earth?
* What is my dog really thinking?
* Do we ever really get to see again people who have died?
* Where does the universe end?
* Will there ever be peace in the world?
* Are any people who say they can tell your future authentic?
* What would it be like to be as brilliant as Steven Hawking was?
* What does it feel like for a baby inside the womb?
* What does dying feel like?
* Does karma really exist?

What are some of life's larger questions that might help spark your sense of wonder?

What could be the benefits of curiosity for you personally?

How could curiosity be beneficial in your relationships with others?

What does being curious say about a person?

When you are not initially curious about something, do you turn away out of disinterest? Become critical of it? Or, are you able to find a spark of curiosity about this new territory?

Einstein was asked how he became so smart. He responded by saying, "I have no special talent. I am only passionately curious." Do you know anyone else like this?

Two key words when thinking about curiosity are "ask" and "listen." Do you think they are important? Explain why.

Reflections

_____

_____

_____

_____

_____

_____

_____

_____

_____

_____

_____

_____

_____

_____

After We Die

Something less
Something more?
We just do not know
What to expect,
What is in store.

When we succumb,
Do we cease to exist,
Becoming as we once were
Before we were born
A notion, a consideration,
Only this
And nothing more?

Or are we off to meet our maker
And then like a candle
Burn down
Making no sound
Perishing forever?
A terrifying nothingness
In a long, black, empty room
With locked doors and a sense of doom

Or do we move on
Repositioning ourselves
Stepping forward
With outstretched arms
Content and at peace,
Floating in a deep, comfortable cloud

As if sleeping,
An authentic paradise
Of comfort and grandeur
With no fear, no loneliness,
With no troubles, no sorrows, no pain
With no dreams, no regrets, and no shame?

Or do we live on
Refreshed and recycled
Into a new form
Not in disguise
But transformed
An enlightened soul
A spirit guide
With a sense of knowing
And a new vision
Of how to be and
How to appear
If given the choice
And a new voice?

Something less
Something more?
On this let us reflect
And take time to explore.

Chapter 12
Look at Aging, Life, and Death

Scenario 1: Judy is approaching seventy and thinks that she will soon stop working and retire. She has mixed feelings about it and does not know whether to look forward to this time or fear it. When some of her friends retired, they easily found new hobbies, interests, and forms of recreation. Others found it more difficult to adapt to new routines and their loss of social roles. They even lost their sense of personal value in the process. What might you say to Judy as she faces aging and the next phase of her life?

Scenario 2: Nadia, age forty-one, is in her final stages of lung cancer. She absolutely cannot believe that she is about to die. She does not feel that sick, but she does have many emotions at this time. What might she be feeling?

Questions for Discussion

Each stage of life has challenges that come with the potential for fear. What do you think is the biggest mountain you have to climb as you are aging?

What are some obvious physical signs of aging?

Describe some physical issues people face as they age.

Aging today seems more manageable than in the past. Is life easier today than it was for our grandparents? If so, how? If not, how has it become more difficult?

What are some views toward aging? Should we fear or celebrate and embrace aging? List ways aging might be frowned upon. Considered a blessing?

How can people feel better about aging?

What are positive actions that can be taken in senior years?

Are people "senior" citizens or "seasoned" citizens?

In the novel *The Giver*, by Lois Lowry, the elder of the Community is the Giver, for he must hold all the knowledge of the past so that the younger members of society do not carry those burdens. What do you think about that? Is it the job of a senior to shelter the next generations from the pain or confusion of the past? In your judgment, what is the job or responsibility of an elder?

Would you say that the psychology of aging has changed over the years? Do younger people today respect and revere their elders? Do elders revere and respect their adult children?

Do you believe there is a new pressure to be productive in the senior years?

Do you fear being a burden to others as you age?

Death is a subject that frightens many people. Yet, are there benefits of being aware of and accepting that we will one day die? How can talking about death with loved ones be beneficial?

Some people do not want to sustain their life when they feel it is time to die. Do you have an opinion about "dying with dignity?"

What is reincarnation? Some who believe in it say that each of us has a specific task to perform in our lifetime and if we don't complete our work, we will be reincarnated over and over until we complete our task. The goal would be a more loving and pain free world. Do you connect with that thinking?

Some people believe everyone ends up in heaven or hell, depending on their behavior on earth. Besides heaven and hell and reincarnations, are there other belief systems about what happens once we die?

A thought: "The great thing about getting older is that you don't lose all the other ages you've been."
~Madeleine L'Engle, American author of young adult fiction

For a chuckle:
"If you die in an elevator, be sure to push the Up button."
~Sam Levenson, author and comedian

Reflections

_____

_____

_____

_____

_____

_____

_____

_____

_____

_____

_____

_____

_____

_____

_____

Open Spaces

As she walks up the hill,
She sees beyond the stately iron gates
A vast, inviting land beyond the broken logs
Ravaged only by time
That line up below a majestic blue sky.
She breathes in a deep sense of gratitude and awe
And with no one around
Alone in her own open space
She feels overwhelming relief
As she is embraced by the warmth
Of much needed hope.

Chapter 13

Maximize Gratitude

Scenario 1: Suzi became discouraged after a difficult day at work and decided she needed to change the course of her day. She sat down, thought for a few moments, and decided to write a thank you note to someone at work whom she appreciated. She felt so good after writing the note that she decided to do one thank you note a day to someone. How could this be a good plan?

Scenario 2: Marie works at the local market, and after one of the employees is diagnosed with a terrible disease, the manager encourages all employees to donate any amount of money to a particular organization that seeks a cure for the disease. After the fundraising campaign ends, the organization wants to show gratitude to the local market. How could this be accomplished?

Questions for Discussion

What does gratitude mean to you? What are you grateful for?

Many people sit in a social situation and talk about what stresses them out or causes them problems. Think about your day. What is the best thing that has happened today? How does talking about that make you feel and change your outlook for that day?

Describe something that has recently influenced you toward a more grateful outlook?

Describe any modern conveniences that make your life easier or more pleasurable.

How has modern medicine helped you or someone you know well and care about?

Who has been the most positive, influential person in your life? Explain what this person has done. Did you ever tell this person?

Think of and describe a special place that makes you feel filled with gratitude for your life. Is it real or imaginary? Does it matter?

What mistake or failure are you grateful for? What was the lesson in it for you?

Who or what inspires you when you need something to keep you going?

Finish these sentences to reflect your gratitude. List as many as come to mind.
* I am forever grateful for

_____.
* I am grateful that

_____.

What can you do to show appreciation?

What do you gain from feeling gratitude?

How can you show yourself gratitude? Write yourself a private love letter. Start with "Dear (your name)," and continue by saying, "I really want you to know that I appreciate how you _____.

On Thanksgiving, people often think about what makes them thankful. Write a list of what you are grateful for in your life. Revisit your list periodically and add to it.

Read the following affirmation:
Despite my imperfections, I love and accept myself completely.
Could you say that to yourself and truly believe it?

Reflections

_____

_____

_____

_____

_____

_____

_____

_____

_____

_____

_____

_____

Let it Be

Do we have a choice?
Do we have a voice?

Ever wonder if whatever happens is your destiny
Experiencing life as it was predetermined to be?

Freewill means you are in control
Fun times can follow your desires to just rock and roll.

Go for it, be in public and be your own guide
Get to decide, if you want, to just go and hide.

How does it matter what you intend to do,
Hold steady, some say, to the course life will take you.

Is life what you make of it or
Is what you do out of your control and just fated?

Journey ahead with a stream of possibilities
Just see what happens and let it be.

Kindness, Determination, Honesty and Compassion
Knock on their door and welcome them in.

Luck is nearby hoping to penetrate
Life's mysteries filled with choice, destiny and fate.

Chapter 14
Navigate Destiny, Fate, and Luck

Scenario 1: Terry, a retired salesman, and his partner planned a cruise with two other couples. The pair assigned to the middle cabin had to cancel their trip due to a family emergency. In approaching their room, Terry noticed the name on the door of the middle cabin as he was heading next door to his own room. On it was the name of his high school basketball coach. He wondered if it was possible that this is the same person as his coach from thirty-five years ago. Later that afternoon, when looking out his porthole, he peered over the railing and saw that it was, indeed, his coach. Was this his fate, destiny, luck, or what?

Scenario 2: James died in a fire when playing with matches at a construction site with friends when he was a teenager. If he had had different friends and had lived in a different city, would he still have died and in a fire? Fate says yes to both, for the path of his life would have been predetermined. Would his destiny have changed if he had made different choices in friends and activities?

Questions for Discussion

What is fate/destiny? What is luck?

Are we at the whim of luck and destiny?

Every day we have many choices to make. Your decisions could determine the outcome of your life. Does that mean that if you change your mind, you change what happens? Or, are there so many things beyond our comprehension? Imagine if you were a parakeet and the only world you know is the world of your cage; yet, there is SO much more out there.

If we feel we make conscious choices are in control, does that mean that if we also believe in destiny, we must not really have any control? Are destiny and control two sides of the same coin?

Is life a random series of events, not predetermined? Or, is predetermination our destiny?

English poet William Ernest Henley wrote about free will in "Invictus":

> Out of the night that covers me,
> Black as the pit from pole to pole,
> I thank whatever gods may be
> For my unconquerable soul.

Henley then concludes, "I am the master of my fate, I am the captain of my soul." Do you believe in free will rather than in destiny, fate, or luck? Do you think you are the "captain of your soul"? Are you and you alone responsible for your own actions and the results that follow?

Do you believe in coincidences?

What control do you have over the people around you? That is, if you are angry, will you attract angry people? If you are happy, will you attract people of the same disposition? Is that fate? Luck? Is your control coming from your own consciousness?

Some might say that people today could be characterized by their use of electronics and conspicuous consumption. Do you think they are not being mindful of what they are doing or where in life they are going? Is that then their destiny?

What conclusions can you draw?

Reflections

PART 2

Improve Your Relationships

Do You Think As I Do?

What do you expect
When you are about to meet someone new?
For them to engage in conversation
And get to know you?

What if they don't seem to notice
You standing nearby
Does your mind then go racing
And you just ask yourself why?

Do you expect others
To think as you do
And get disappointed or walk away
When you see it is not true?

Sometimes our expectations
Are unrealistic or unreasonable
And our disappointment that follows
Truly unbelievable.

If we look at our expectations
And change them here and there
Maybe we will find
Others really do care.

People just have their own way
When they respond and react
Relationships are not automatically smooth
And that's an undeniable fact.

Chapter 15

Observe the Expectations of Others and Learn When to Let Go of Your Expectations

Scenario 1: When James and his sister were younger, she always treated him like he was a pest. James, now 45, cannot forgive his sister, because, as he sees it, she treated him like he did not matter when they were children. Even as adults, she never seems interested in his life. He is bitter and expects more. Now she suddenly wants a loving relationship with her brother but he cannot let go of their past relationship. How might you respond to James' plight?

Scenario 2: Tiffany talks of her resentment toward her mother, who she is convinced loved her brother more than her when they were children. The relationship with her mother eventually improves and gives Tiffany a feeling of being loved, yet the memory of her childhood does not go away. How should Tiffany handle this dilemma?

Scenario 3: You are at the supermarket in the express line, a place where twelve items or less is set up for checkout. A middle-aged woman cuts in front of you with at least twenty-five items and says, "Don't worry. I'll be quick." What do you say/do?

Questions for Discussion

Can you forgive and just let go of your anger, hurt, or grudge? Does it depend on the transgression?

What are some outcomes of being angry? What may be an advantage of letting go of anger?

What can you say or do to help yourself let go? Can you forgive without condoning or excusing what the offender did?

What general expectations do you have of others? Are they realistic? High? Low? What happens when you hold on to expectations of others too long?

Are you a perfectionist?

Do you think most people follow their own path or follow a path based on the expectations of society or others?

Are there times when one must be a perfectionist?

What do you expect of others? Complete the following:
* I expect my friend to
  _____.
* I expect my children to
  _____.

What would happen if you let go of your expectations of others?

Consider:
- ✶ Do you expect forgiveness or do you tend to ask for forgiveness?
- ✶ Do you expect things to happen as you wish if you have put in your best effort?
- ✶ Do you expect to win when competing? Does it depend on who your opponent is…a child, a partner, close friend, a stranger?

What happens when someone you consider a "best friend" no longer seems to be a "safe" friend that you can completely trust and know has your best interest in mind always? You no longer feel close or trusting of this friend. How do you handle this? Do you dismiss the friendship? Lower your expectations of the friend? Or, do you talk it out, for you only know what is in your head and you do not know the other point of view? What is the risk involved in broaching this subject with your friend?

Is it good to have high expectations of others? When? When can it be detrimental?

Should we expect others to return favors? If they do, not, should we be disappointed?

Expectations can be reasonable; yet, who defines reasonable? Is an attitude of "good enough" a healthier way to look at one's life experiences?

People often get caught up in what should or should not

happen, what someone might or might not do. That takes up a lot of energy. Do you sometimes feel disappointed by other people or events that happen because of your expectations? If you do, how do you handle that?

Are expectations higher today for children? Many parents expect perfection or at least a better version of themselves from their children. Do you think that "good enough" should be considered an option for an expectation of a child? Does that depend on one's age? Would an attitude of "good enough" be a realistic expectation for a senior citizen who, upon trying to get up from a seated position and holding on to something, thinks to himself, "At least I can still get up"?

"Lowering your expectations" sounds negative. Is it? How could you lower your expectations and make that a positive move? Are there some expectations that should not be lowered?

Is having expectations (real or imagined) a healthy way to conduct your life?

When given a choice and you do not want to follow the majority, do you feel obligated to go along rather than follow your heart? What could the advantage be if you followed your heart rather than the desires of others at that moment?

What else (besides things) do people need to let go of in order to achieve their personal goals?

Take an inventory of what you need to let go of. What does that include?

Susan Fay West, author and certified organizer coach, advises, "The mental and physical space we create by letting go of things that belong in our past gives us the option to fill the space with something new."
Have you let go of some things in order to let in something new to your life? Describe how that might look.

Reflections

Hand In Hand

If you are a parent, then be one.
Guide, model, and follow through
Do as I say and
Do as I do.

Firmness, consistency,
Boundaries within reason.
Consequences for actions.
If you are a parent, then be one.

A positive attitude
A caring heart
A confident grasp
Of right and wrong
From the start.

Enter the child's world
Its magic and mystery.
Exit together slowly,
Hand in hand
Into reality.

Chapter 16
Practice and Prioritize Responsibility

Scenario 1: John recently graduated from college and was fortunate to find an internship at a law firm. When he lost a client file, he told no one and acted as if he had never seen the file. What was he risking? If he had admitted he had misplaced the file, what might he have gained? Was this an issue of responsibility, honesty, fear, or a combination?

Scenario 2: Your teenage daughter Marsha is seventeen now. Since she was six years old, she has had four girlfriends, all from respectable families. They are all nice girls and all of them have grown up spending a great deal of time together. However, at seventeen, Marsha has drifted away from this group and now spends time with two girls who are unsupervised, wild, and prone to getting into trouble in school. What do you do as a parent in this situation?

Questions for Discussion

Responsibility is being accountable for something within your power. What is a child under ten responsible for? A teenager? An adult? A senior? Be specific.

Do we have responsibilities in our family? Are these self-imposed or expected?

What responsibilities do we have in our role as a good friend?

A friend of yours is stuck in the anger stage of grieving over the loss of a dear one. Are you responsible to help your friend in this situation?

To avoid taking responsibility for something, what excuses have you heard people use?
* I was too

  _____.

* I can't

  _____.

What is the effect of placing blame on someone? Consider two adults in a household. Upon arriving home, one of them sees damage to the fender of the other's car. A yelling match ensues about the damaged car and the carelessness that led to it. What might have been another way for them to handle this?

What are some things you have no control over? Complete this sentence: I have little control over

_____ and _____.

If you have little control over these things, do you still feel responsible for them happening? Should you?

Who is responsible for your success and well-being? Your parents? Your partner or spouse? Your boss? Only you? The world at large? Luck? Some of each?

Are expectations cultural? If so, be specific. For example, if you are an adult living in China, what and who are you responsible for?

Do we have a societal responsibility to another society's suffering? Explain your position on this.

Reflections

Apparent Contradictions

Think about praise and criticism,
Both can be realistic,
Both can be wounding.
Indeed, how do they differ
Just what can you infer?

Do you smile when you are praised?
Do you frown when put down?
Can you also be saved by criticism
Or ruined by praise?
We choose how to respond
Sometimes appalled, sometimes amazed.

Chapter 17

Quiet or Quell Criticism:
Constructive, Destructive

Scenario 1: Tom's mother said, "You never put your clothes away in the hamper at the end of the day, and your room is always such a mess with the clothes everywhere. I can't stand it!" After this destructive criticism, Tom mutters something under his breath and says it is his room and to leave him alone. What could his mother have said to make it more constructive and generate the response she had probably hoped for?

Scenario 2: Sharon is in a singing competition and asks Marion for her opinion of her rehearsal performance. Marion says it was nice but that her voice cracks on the high notes and her low notes are a bit too throaty and off pitch. Sharon's feelings are hurt. Why? How could Marion have handled her criticism differently?

Questions for Discussion

You may have heard someone say, "I need a thicker skin. I am just too sensitive when someone criticizes me." Does criticism have to be taken personally? If so, why? If not, how can it be taken?

Sometimes we begin a comment or criticism with "I." Sometimes we begin with "You." How does the choice of wording on a job, a specific behavior, or a mishap around the house affect the outcome?

Why do people tend to become defensive when being criticized?

Is there anything positive about criticism? What opportunities can result from constructive criticism? How can it give you an advantage?

What is the difference between constructive and destructive criticism?

People will often avoid giving constructive criticism out of fear that they do not know how to do it. What are some ways you can give people constructive criticism?

Would it help to focus on the situation rather than the person?

When we criticize others, it could come from a dark side of our personality and feel like an attack to the person we criticize. What would such negative sides of our personality be rooted in? Are we broken and get a sense of superiority when we tear others down?

How important is the source when you feel you have been the victim of destructive criticism?

How can you turn destructive criticism to your advantage?

Can you choose whom you will listen to?

Can you control what a person will say to you? How?

Can you control how you react to criticism? How?

Norman Vincent Peale, author of *The Power of Positive Thinking,* stated, "The trouble with most of us is that we would rather be ruined by praise than saved by criticism." Do you think that is true of most people?

How do you feel about criticism from people you consider smart? Can you think of a time when someone gave you constructive criticism that you found useful?

According to Illinois Senator Dick Durbin, it is challenging to "run for public office and face an opponent, to decide on issues, what is the best thing, then face the criticism from colleagues, voters, the press and defend yourself." Do you believe people know how to respond to criticism, whether constructive or destructive? Explain.

Reflections

_____

_____

_____

_____

_____

_____

_____

_____

_____

_____

_____

_____

_____

_____

My Special Princess and the Princess in Me

Do princesses always wear a sparkling crown
Or wave a scepter to be heard?
Smile at excited crowds
Save a gosling or an injured bird?
My princess wears jewels in her heart
Bravely smiling as she faces roads rarely traveled.
An inspiration to me as my daily routines
Unravel amidst everyday redirections.

Her inner essence, a glimpse into her soul,
Powerful, magical, at once a beam of life
A moment later eclipsed by darkness
And always emerging as the princess
Who proudly and bravely wears her special crown.

She makes me look inside myself
To find the everyday strength
To be the better me that
I hope you can see.

Today I will be a princess
Wear a brilliant crown and bravely
Face any obstacles in my way
And like my princess
See them, walk by them, and move forward always.

Chapter 18

Reaffirm Friendship During Challenging Times

Scenario 1: Your dear friend Debbie was recently diagnosed with an extremely serious illness. You have never been in this situation before and are not exactly sure what to say or do. What can you say when you call her? What gestures can you make to show that you are thinking of her? How do you proceed?

Scenario 2: Your friend's husband was caught having an affair with someone at his place of business. You have always felt uneasy around him and have suspected that he was always friendly but controlled. You have been friends with them as a couple, and now that his affair is public knowledge, you feel you have to choose who to maintain a supportive friendship with...him or his wife. How can this be challenging?

Questions for Discussion

Have you ever had a friend pull away from you because of a personal difficulty? Why do you think your friend pulled away? Do people need "space" sometimes? How should you navigate your friendship if you think your friend is going through something painful, humiliating, or embarrassing?

Have you ever avoided someone to escape involvement in a difficulty that the person was going through? Why did you do it and how did this make you feel? Did you consider how this would be received or interpreted by your friend?

Bad "stuff" happens. How do you help a friend move forward? What can a person say to open a dialogue with someone who is suffering without offering advice?

Give five supportive comments one could make to someone who is hurting. What could you say to show empathy?

Give five gestures of kindness and understanding. Is a silent presence an option?

What should you "not" do?

What comments might be inappropriate to say?

Friendship may be fragile during a challenging time. It has often been compared to glass or china. Consider the following concept: True friendship is like china, for it is valuable and rare. Once it gets broken, it can be put back together but the crack remains.
Do you agree?

Sometimes bad things happen to you as well. What can you do to be your own best friend? What conversation can you have with yourself?

Reflections

Who's to Blame?

I can't, I won't,
I'm afraid, I didn't

Purposely trick you, drop you,
Go that high, let you fall.

You shouldn't, you didn't
You dropped me, you let go.

I, I, you, you
Didn't, wouldn't, shouldn't.

Let's try to trust one another
Let's become a We.

Chapter 19
Scrutinize Trust and Betrayal

Scenario 1: One day, when Sarah was having a conversation with her best friend Margo, she shared one of her darkest secrets. Later that day, without thinking about it, Margo mentioned it to an acquaintance they both knew. When do you talk about what a friend has privately shared with you? When does it become gossip? Should Margo tell Sarah she mentioned it to someone? If so, how should Sarah handle this apparent betrayal?

Scenario 2: Erin has worked at a firm for two years and has, in her mind, become a trusted friend of Agnes. Erin has a strong sense that the insurance company she is working for is not as up-to-date as it should be about the security of customer account information. She shares her thoughts with Agnes, whom she trusts implicitly to keep this a private conversation. The next week, Erin's boss calls her in for a meeting and informs her that Agnes shared the conversation about security. Should Erin feel betrayed? What are ways she can handle this?

How do you know when you have a friend you can trust? What qualities might that other person have?

Do you have an intuitive guide within you that leads you to recognize who is and who is not trustworthy?

How can a betrayal occur in a friendship? In a marriage? In a business?

The severe breach of trust, betrayal, can cause serious distress. What emotions are involved in a betrayal? What possible effects are there of betrayal?

What are some ways to handle a betrayal?

Imagine the stars in a solar system and how their positions can change, placing them further away at times. Now think about friendships. Once someone, on more than one occasion, is unkind to a friend, a level of trust is gone and an emotional distance develops, placing them further away from each other. Can the friend who was betrayed still feel safe with that "friend"? What happens to trust in that situation? Can one learn to trust again? Should that "friend" be trusted again?

Sometimes you might have to assess the probability of betrayal. What might be the benefits of trusting someone again who has previously betrayed you?

Is betrayal an intentional act? That is, if someone betrays you, must you conclude it was intentional?

Friedrich Nietzsche said, "I'm not upset that you lied to me, I'm upset that from now on I can't believe you." Would you agree with him?

When you have been let down by someone, you have to ask yourself if trying to trust that person again is worth the risk. How will you decide? How does one learn to trust again?

Do past experiences determine your level of trust in others? How so?

Consider this: Do you have the qualities, motives, and actions that others can rely on? Are you loyal and believable? If you are not sure, would you be willing to ask some of your friends?

Is there such a thing as "sort of trustworthy"?

Reflections_____

_____

_____

_____

_____

_____

_____

_____

_____

_____

_____

_____

_____

_____

The Voice of Forgiving

If someone intends to cause you harm
Using complete deception to hurt you
It reflects their stupidity, hostility, and malice
In the injustice that ensues.

If someone unwittingly hurts you
With no intent in mind
It undoubtedly still causes considerable pain.
It is a mistake of another kind.

What words and thoughts follow
When you feel you have been wronged,
Out flow blame, resentment, anger and depression,
You then feel betrayed and dismayed
From the loss of this personal connection.

Consider forgiveness and feelings of calm,
Found in a truce of recognizing
The need to each move forward
Using mutual voices of understanding.

Chapter 20

Try Forgiveness

Scenario 1: Your boss publicly derides you at a meeting of twelve of your peers and basically shuts you down. How can you take steps to not only get past this incident but also to forgive your boss? Should you forgive your boss?

Scenario 2: A husband and wife drive home from an evening with friends. The husband is exhausted and falls asleep at the wheel, causing the vehicle to veer off the road, and crash into a tree at sixty mph. Fortunately, both survive the crash. He is minimally injured, but his wife is very seriously injured. How does she feel and what might go through her mind as she lays in the hospital for weeks?

Scenario 3: Imagine you and your partner are close friends with three other couples. One plans a vacation and invites the other two couples to join them. You and your partner are not included and you feel slighted. Do you bring it up to the couple planning the getaway? Do you think this will affect your friendship? Do you forgive them? Should this be about forgiveness?

Questions for Discussion

What kinds of words, gestures, or wrongdoings by others lead you to feelings of anger? Do an inventory and be specific about one moment when you have been angry and have been holding a grudge. You would like to forgive that person for the indiscretion. What does your conversation with yourself look like? Specifically, if you have to forgive someone, how do you do it? What do you say to yourself? What do you say to that person?

We all make mistakes. In a relationship, do you think that we each own some of every situation? Or, are there times when one person could be completely at fault?

How can you release yourself of your anger and resentment? What do you say to yourself? Complete the following sentence starters:

* I wish that

  _____.

* I release

  _____.

* I want to

  _____.

What are some specific ways you can show your forgiveness?

Is it easier to forgive a friend or a family member?

Some say to live in love rather than to inflict harm. What do you think about that?

What do you think are the benefits of forgiveness?

What are the effects of refusing to find forgiveness?

Is forgiveness all or nothing or are there varying degrees?

Ancient Chinese philosopher Confucius stated, "To be wronged is nothing, unless you continue to remember it." What did he mean?

Author of children and adult fiction Isabelle Holland gives this insight: "As long as you don't forgive, who and whatever it is will occupy a rent-free space in your mind." Is that really what you want when you refuse to forgive someone? Who wins? Who loses?

Who is forgiveness ultimately for? Discuss the possibilities.

Reflections_____

_____

_____

_____

_____

_____

_____

_____

_____

_____

_____

_____

_____

_____

_____

Deciding What to Say or Do

Political candidates share their intentions
As they campaign,
But who can know what is behind their words?
Are they facts, observations, or personal judgments
Can we tell from what we have just heard?

A company has rules and expectations
That are either followed or broken
Do you, an employee seeing it all,
Judge others for wrongful acts that remain unspoken?

What counts more...a person's actions or intent?
So much for us to each consider
As we listen and decide all day long.
Should we investigate and verify or simply infer?

Do people judge and speak to you
Based on their own life experiences,
Or are their comments based on facts
Or a self-serving need to feel victorious?

Feeling judged can be exhausting,
As you react and decide what to say and do,
Sensing you are often being watched and judged
Can be daunting or encouraging...it is really up to you.

Think about the one doing the judging.
Who is right or suffering in their own personal pain?
You can feel hurt or feel compassion.
From the latter what might you gain?

We all judge others from time to time.
Are your thoughts all justifiable?
Or, perhaps it best to view what is worthy
And hold dear the good that is undeniable.

Chapter 21

Unpopularize Judging Others

Scenario 1: You are out with friends. A slightly younger woman walks in and is inappropriately dressed. She notices you all snickering at her and one of you rolling your eyes at her. When you think about it now, how does this make you feel about yourself and your friends' reactions?

Scenario 2: Your son is about to be married and you are sharing the expense with the bride's parents. Due to limited space and event coordination, your son and his fiancé tell you that you may invite fifteen relatives. You have at least twenty-five you want to invite. How do you handle explanations with the ones not invited? Do you expect them to judge you?

Scenario 3: At church or temple, the person next to you, a twenty-five to thirty-year-old you do not know, starts to text during the sermon. How do you respond? React? How do you show your judgment? What are your body's feelings or sensations when you judge others?

Questions for Discussion

What happens when a close friend does something unkind more than once? Does it feel right to alter how you feel about that person?

What are some reasons we judge others?

Scottish author and poet Robert Louis Stevenson advised, "Don't judge each day by the harvest you reap but by the seeds that you plant."
What did he mean?

Think about someone you know whose behavior you have in the past judged in a negative light. What were your criticisms of this person? Now, think about something you could say about this person that is positive. What would it be?

Imagine going through this thought process in your head the next time you are tempted to judge someone in a harsh manner. How might you benefit from thinking (to yourself) something positive about the person you are quick to criticize and saying nothing out loud?

What are some other ways to stop judging others?

What is the difference between judging others and observing without judgment? What is the challenge involved?

Swiss psychiatrist and psychoanalyst Carl Jung taught that "Everything that irritates us about others can lead us to an understanding of ourselves." How might what we think or feel about someone help us personally?

Reflections

Space and Time

When your computer crashes or a car
nearly sideswipes you,
Or your co-worker makes a mistake,
causing you lost time,
The choice of how to proceed
is yours for such disruptive misdeeds.

You can react and yell, get outraged,
gesture indignantly,
Have a sharp retort, shout hurtful, reactive words
Or be rigid in place, starring steely-eyed ahead
Quietly seething with nothing said.

Or, you can pause to breathe it all in.
Consider the circumstances at hand,
And use space and time and your inner voice
Responding with self-control may be the best choice.

Chapter 22

Verbalize When Responding and Reacting
What is the difference?

Scenario 1: You leave the town where you live to visit the city where you grew up and make plans to get together with family and friends from your childhood. As a courtesy, you call a relative who has been busy when you have visited in the past, hoping that this time you will meet. Your relative says, regretfully, that she cannot meet you because she has an appointment all afternoon. That day, you see this relative at a mall, and she is loaded with packages she has bought. What do you do? What do you say?

Scenario 2: You are at a store and a clerk seems to be in a bad mood or irritated. Would you say anything in "reaction" to his/her unfriendliness or rudeness or pretend to ignore it and just complete your purchase? What could you say in a "response" that might be an energy changer for that person?

Scenario 3: On your flight to Chicago, a woman sits next to you in the center seat and she begins to eat a Reuben sandwich. It is so large and messy that the corned beef and sauerkraut, along with the Russian dressing, shoot all over your outfit. What do you say and do?

Questions for Discussion

We have all heard and probably said the following:
Think before you speak.
Do we do that?

Viktor E. Frankl, a prominent Jewish psychologist who survived two concentration camps, explains in his book, *Man's Search for Meaning*, "Between stimulus and response there is a space. In that space is our power to choose our response. In our response lies our growth and our freedom."
What has to happen to turn a reaction into a response? Is time a factor? Or, is it the trigger behind the two different actions?

What is the difference between "reacting" and "responding"? For example, which is rational and which is irrational? Conscious or instinctual?

What could you say to someone who has hurt your feelings or said something you consider rude? What language would you use in "reaction" to what that person said? Could there be any benefit in asking the person to explain their intent before you reacted? Would your language be different if you would have initially paused to consider the situation?

What if you think you deserve their rudeness? What can you do or say?

Could an insensitive remark or insult to you result from a person's suffering or something that has nothing to do with you? If so, should you react or respond?

How can you respond to negative people?

How can you take back your own negative reaction or turn it into something constructive?

When is an immediate, kneejerk reaction appropriate?

According to Eleanor Roosevelt, "No one can make you feel inferior without your consent." What is more likely to make you feel inferior, a reaction or a response? Explain.

Do you think perception is as powerful as reality? Can someone be unkind through their facial expression? Can a facial expression be both a reaction and a response?

> **For a chuckle**: "Before you marry a person, you should first make them use a computer with slow internet service to see who they really are."
> ~Will Ferrell, actor and comedian

Reflections

The ABC's of Success

Accomplish a goal
Bolster someone's self-esteem
Control your temper
Do your best
Earn the respect of others
Fix what is broken
Give from the heart
Help someone with a task
Initiate a conversation
Just be yourself
Kiss a loved one
Let go of what pains you
Make a difference in the life of others
Never give up
Overcome a fear
Provide friendship to someone in need
Question your motives
Read and complete a good book
Solve a problem
Take charge when needed
Understand before reacting
Validate the feelings of another
Write a thank you note
X-out your negative feelings
Yell for joy
Zero in on what matters.

Remind yourself today
That no size fits all,
What truly matters
Is completely your call.

Chapter 23
Working for Success

Scenario 1: A sanitation worker has a weekly route in your neighborhood, and residents are required to take their garbage cans to the curb the night before pick up. James has been on this route for years and notices that Mrs. Mackey, an elderly widow, does not have her garbage out. He exits his truck and takes out her cans, though he is breaking company rules. What do you think of his personal dedication? Is he successful in his job?

Scenario 2: You have twin teenaged daughters, and you are so proud of their accomplishments in piano and violin. It has been a busy year at work, though, and you have not been able to attend their recitals; you have, however, seen videos of them. At work you have just received a bonus and compliments via a public announcement in the company newsletter for closing the largest business deal in five years. Your boss and associates are completely impressed. Do you feel successful?

Questions for Discussion

What determines success? Is your success defined only by yourself or by others? Some societies tend to gauge success based upon wealth. Can you be successful without wealth?

Consider other cultures. What are some of their measures of success?

Do you see a difference between being highly regarded and being successful?

Achieving success depends on the age and stage of your life. What is the evidence you might have observed in a child who appears to feel successful at something? For a young adult from twenty to thirty? For someone forty to sixty? For a senior?

In Man's Search for Meaning, Viktor E. Frankl discusses success as follows:

> Success, like happiness, cannot be pursued; it must ensue, and it only does so as the unintended side-effect of one's personal dedication to a cause greater than oneself or as the by-product of one's surrender to a person other than oneself; they took everything away from me, but they couldn't take away my dignity.

What does he mean? What are ways we can achieve success without making success our goal?

Think of someone you know who you feel is a success. Why is that person truly successful?

Do you feel you are a success? In what ways? In what ways do you feel you are not successful? Are you doing something to change that?

Is feeling successful a building block to future successes? If so, how?

Joshua Becker, bestselling author of *The More of Less*, writes in the post, "Becoming Minimalist," that we need to rewrite our measurements of success. He suggests we consider such situations as how we behave when alone, face difficulties, treat others, deal with authority, and handle ourselves when we make a mistake. What do you think of his advice?

A thought: "If you try to fail, and succeed, which have you done?"
~George Carlin, comedian

Another thought: "I think everybody should get rich and famous and do everything they ever dreamed of so they can see that it's not the answer."
~Jim Carrey, comedian

And one more thought: "When you're not concerned with succeeding, you can work with complete freedom."
~Larry David, writer, producer, and actor

Reflections

Dare to Care

I look so much better with make-up, you say?
And it is nice to see me make an effort today?

Who are you, a boss, a spouse, or a so-called friend
Whose unkind remarks need to end?

Nothing to be gained from unkindness, you see
Meanness and insults just should not be.

Look for the goodness, it is always there
For us all to find if we really do care.

Treasure the heart that offers a smile of trust
Enjoy a safe feeling inside that is always a must.

Chapter 24

X-out Over-reacting to an Unkind or Uncomplimentary Remark

Scenario 1: Grandpa Henry and Grandma Henrietta go to the Saturday matinee movie and wait in line to buy tickets. When their turn comes to purchase their tickets, they say to the young man behind the counter, "Two senior tickets, please." He responds, "No kidding." How might they react?

Scenario 2: You are at a restaurant, you order food, and it comes out uncooked. You send it back. The waitress seems annoyed. After close to fifteen minutes, she brings it back, and it is not what you ordered. You point this out, and she slams it on the table saying, "Take it or leave it." What do you say or do?

Questions for Discussion

Some of us grew up being advised by our parents to ignore insulting or painful words said to us by others. "Sticks and stones may break my bones, but words will never hurt me," they would quote.

Yet, words can be very hurtful. "Words have energy and power with the ability to help, to heal, to hinder, to hurt, to harm, to humiliate and to humble," according to Yehuda Berg, the author and spiritual director of The Kabbalah Children's Academy.

Think of a time when someone said something to you that you felt was uncalled for. What do you remember and how did it impact you?

How do you tend to react or respond as an adult to an unkind remark? Do you over-react? What would that look like if you did?

What might be healthy ways to respond to insulting words? For example, imagine that a friend tells you that a mutual acquaintance has said something negative about you, and you quickly feel very surprised and hurt. You could play this over and over in your mind for days, confront the person who made the unkind remark, or consider that it was not really personal but rather a symptom of that person having had a bad day and choose to put it behind you. Have you experienced this and if so, how have you managed it?

Would any of these be your response to an unkind remark?
* Can you help me understand what is going on here?
* Why are you talking to me like this?
* What happened to cause you to want to hurt me by insulting me?
* You are delusional!

What are some other possible responses?

What could you take into consideration when someone says something mean to you?

Christine Carter, Ph.D., author and Senior Fellow at the Greater Good Science Center, suggests the following in the article, "How to Deal with Mean People," (April 15, 2013):

> ...fight fire with *water* by sending loving thoughts to the people who hurt you...I use a traditional loving-kindness meditation, and say

things like 'May you be happy. May you be healthy and strong. May you be free from suffering' while imagining the person who tried to hurt me.

Would you consider doing this? How might it help you cope with being the victim of a cruel comment?

What about the disguised insult? It is an insult wrapped in a compliment. Can you recall being the recipient of this?

Sometimes you may be the perpetrator rather than the victim of a hurtful remark. According to ancient Greek philosopher Socrates, "If what you want to say is neither true, nor good or kind, nor useful or necessary, please don't say anything at all." Would you agree with this? Could you take a moment to consider what you are about to say before saying it? Would you? Do you think people know when something will be cruel but tend to go ahead and say it anyway?

What if what you are considering saying is true yet could sound harsh? Should you, then, say something directly to the person anyway? What do you need to consider first?

Could you apologize and say, "I am sorry," if you unintentionally said something mean to someone? Or, would it come out like this:
"I am sorry, but …" as you go on and try to explain why you said it? How do you apologize?

Reflections

_____

_____

_____

_____

_____

_____

_____

_____

_____

_____

_____

_____

_____

_____

_____

_____

_____

_____

_____

_____

Listen Up, Down, Across and Around

Hear it
Consider it
Imagine it
Acknowledge it.
Question it
Evaluate it.
Understand it.
Critique it.
Contradict it.
Praise it.
Admit it.
Adopt it.
Never ignore it.

Chapter 25
Yes to Listening

Scenario 1: Barbara comes home from work terribly frustrated. She approaches her husband in his home office and vents her frustration, saying she gets absolutely no respect at the office and has been given no chance to advance. She feels that she is at a crisis point with work. He does not look up from his computer but tells her he understands and feels so sorry this is happening. Was he hearing her or listening? Is this how you would want someone to respond?

Scenario 2: Robs spends the afternoon with a friend he has not seen for some time. Rob begins sharing a recent exciting experience. Rob's friend interrupts saying, "You think that's something? Let me tell you what happened to me last week!" Rob was talking before being interrupted, but was his friend listening? What might Rob be thinking?

Questions for Discussion

Do you think people like talking more than listening? Explain your answer.

What is the difference between the act of hearing and active listening? Would you describe yourself as an active or passive listener?

Do you give a person who is speaking eye contact when you are engaged in a conversation?

What gives you the sense at times that people are hearing you but not listening to what you are saying?

Might people be thinking about their own response or their own viewpoint when someone is speaking rather than listening? How can you tell?

One of the great American 20th century novelists, Ernest Hemingway, instructed, "When people talk, listen completely. Most people never listen." Would you agree with him?

Do you think that most people remember what they hear? Do most people pay attention to what they do not agree with? If we hear something that opposes our notions, convictions, and deeply rooted prejudices, do we mentally "tune out," plan a rebuttal and stop listening?

Eighteenth century French writer Voltaire noted, "The best way to become boring is to say everything." How do you handle situations you are in when someone dominates the environment? Do you interrupt? Do you walk away? What are other options?

Advances in technology are supposed to help with communication. What effect do you think the progress of modern technology has had on the ability of people to have a conversation?

For a chuckle: "I'm always relieved when someone is delivering a eulogy and I realize I'm listening to it."
~George Carlin, comedian, actor and author

A thought: "Congress is so strange. A man gets up to speak and says nothing, nobody listens and then everybody disagrees."
~Will Rogers, American humorist, newspaper columnist, and actor

Reflections

As I Looked Around, What Did I See

Long ago, on rocks surrounded
By a vista of lush mountains,
Diamonds of sun-filled light sparkled brilliantly
As they reflected off the lake resting in the middle.
Majestic beauty abounded all around
Serenity, Total Peace, and Ecstasy.
I looked and took it all in
This moment of awe and wonder
Always there for me to relive and call upon forever.

Chapter 26
Zoom in to Truly See

Scenario 1: Eric is a coach of an 8-year old girls' soccer team playing its fourth game of the season. One of his players has never played before this season and struggles to make contact with the ball. Eric watches as her emotions overtake her and she rubs her eyes crying. What could he do?

Scenario 2: Sheila goes on a vacation and plans to visit the Louvre Museum in Paris. When she looks up in one of the rooms, her eyes find the famous painting, the Mona Lisa. When she gets closer, though, she sees that Da Vinci's masterpiece is not only painted on a wood plank rather than canvas, but also blends all the colors so subtly that she cannot even see clear lines where one color ends and another begins. Do you think people usually mechanically look at what is around them or take the time to "see" what is around them?

Questions for Discussion

What is the difference between looking and seeing?

In today's fast paced life, we look at things and people all day long. Do we really see them? We use our vision, yes, but do we go further and try to understand what we see? Do we pay attention? How observant are we of our surroundings?

Consider this advice from the German philosopher Friedrich Nietzsche:

> Look back upon your life and ask: What up to now have you truly loved, what has raised your soul, what ruled it and at the same time made

you happy? Line up these objects of reverence before you, and see how they form a ladder on which you have so far climbed up toward your true self.

What does Nietzsche want you to be able to do?

Think about meeting someone for the first time. You look at that person, and that person looks at you. Knowing that first impressions are important, what would you like this person to see when looking at you? How would you like them to complete the following sentences?

* I see that

_____.

* I see how

_____.

* I see your

_____.

How would you complete the sentences when you truly see the person standing across from you?

* I see that

_____.

* I see how

_____.

* I see your

_____.

What shapes and drives how you see the world?

Think of a third world country. How do you think the residents "see" their world of poverty, economic instability and inadequate human necessities such as access to water, shelter or food?

Think about on-line communication today. People often do not hear or see the person with whom they are communicating, as they are corresponding through emails, texts or a voice. What might they be missing by not "seeing" each other?

Fortunately, with the many video chat applications available today, people can view the facial expressions and reactions during a conversation that takes place remotely. How does that compare to person-to-person communication?

Poet and American essayist Henry David Thoreau summarized it all by stating, "It's not what you look at that matters, it's what you see."

Reflections

Epilogue, Afterword, Outward, Last Shot

Our Wisdom Walk

We came together
Some already as dear friends,
Some as acquaintances,
Others as momentary strangers,

Sharing thoughts,
Insights that may delight
Move us, surprise us,
Make us wonder,

Threaded together
As weavers of wisdom,
Our own community
Nourishing who we really were
Or hoped to become.

We talked
Some openly,
Some with reserve,
Others in silence with a velvet heart,
About forgiveness, self-love, expectations
Energy fueled by gratitude, appreciation of life's
simplest gestures,
Authenticity, Integrity, Living Mindfully,
Observing without judgment,
Reminding ourselves that like attracts like
And to reflect on our did wells each and every day,

About giving off goodness that generates more
goodness in another
So that it would become our reality
Leaving no room for energy that could deplete us all.

We began to step
A little lighter yet more thoughtfully,
Off to create a time of stillness
From a textured life of many patterns
As we went on our own personal wisdom walk
To think about the person within.

Acknowledgements

I wish to thank some special people for their encouragement, support, and guidance from my initial concept through the process of writing this book.

As I embarked on this journey, Melanie Steiner, you gave me initial help with the overall organization of my topics. Patty Briggs, thank you for looking at several early drafts and making suggestions on ways to make the material user-friendly and consistent in tone. Ellen Fischer, as an author yourself, you wisely encouraged me to make myself knowledgeable about the process of writing to publish. Judy Mansfield and Linda Stamer, thank you for your kind friendship and careful scrutiny of the thinking involved in each chapter. To Kat Chapman Steuer and Arlene Bice, thank you for your ruby-toned wisdom and honesty. Jill Chapin, friend and fellow author, thank you for your expertise in editing, as well as to Dr. Pam Sirota for your professional wisdom and editing guidance.

Finally, many thanks to my husband Ken, who steadfastly remained not only completely supportive at every step but always reminded me to stand up and stretch after hours at my computer.

Author Page

Vicki Silverman grew up in St. Louis, Missouri, where she began her career as a high school English teacher. She has since been living in Los Angeles and has taught English and public speaking to high school, middle school, and elementary age children. Her lists of questions on each topic in this book fit her teacher-at-heart non-fiction side, while her poetry reflects her craftsmanship with words.

Along with her husband Ken, she has also raised two children who now have children of their own. Vicki credits her now grown children Julie and Scott with supplying a wealth of creative problem-solving antics in their youth, which led to the first important "question" Vicki asked herself: Why me?

In her free time, she indulges in a personal passion for reading and writing, as well as projects and volunteer work of all kinds.

She wrote *Questions On Topics That Matter* as an understandable tool for readers to revisit their lives and be excited that there is always room for personal growth, self-awareness, and the end-of-the-day satisfaction that indeed, it has been a good day.

Made in the USA
San Bernardino, CA
22 December 2018